Rumi's Seeds
277 Quotes to Nourish the Heart and Soul

About the Editor

Born in Mexico, Glen Alberto Salazar grew up in California. He holds up a bachelor's degree from UC Berkeley. In addition to writing he enjoys Persian poetry, art, and culture. He currently lives in Northern California.

Also by Glen Alberto Salazar

Splendid Azerbaijan: The History and Culture of the Land of Fire

A Little Book of Persian Poetry

A Little Book of Haiku

Rumi's Seeds

277 quotes to nourish the heart and soul

Glen Alberto Salazar

Nectar Books

Copyright© Glen Alberto Salazar 2018

All rights reserved. Nectar Books.

Cover: Uzhdavini, Galina. *Pomegranates*.

ISBN: 978-1095229439

Book design by Glen Alberto Salazar

Published in the United States of America

10   9   8   7   6   5   4   3   2   1

To all those seeking to nourish their hearts and their souls

as they go through this wonder and mystery we call life!

It's time to speak of roses and pomegranates and of the

ocean where pearls are made.

–Rumi

Contents

Introduction ... 1

277 Rumi Quotes ... 5

Pomegranates from Ancient Persia to California ... 99

The Pomegranate Garden (Poem by Rumi) ... 105

Pomegranate Blossoms (Poem by Rumi) ... 107

Pomegranate Flower Blush (Poem by Rumi) ... 109

The Laughter of Pomegranates (Poem by Rumi) ... 111

Pomegranate Proverbs ... 115

 Introduction

Jalal al-Din Rumi was born on the edge of the Persian Empire, in the city of Balkh, in Greater Khorasan, in what today is Afghanistan, although this is disputed and some argue his birthplace is the village of Wakhsh, in what today is Tajikistan, in 1207. Rumi's family fled persecution and death from the Mongol hordes, finding refuge in the Central Asian city of Samarkand, in present day Uzbekistan, and then in Konya, a city in Anatolia, in present day Turkey. In 1229, his father was invited by the Seljuk Turk sultan to teach theology in the Seljuk capital, Konya. Rumi studied to become a scholar and teacher in Aleppo and Damascus, becoming a disciple of Sayyed

Termazi and learned the spiritual matters and secrets of Sufism, the mystical branch of Islam. In 1231, Rumi became a Sufi master, preaching in the mosques of Konya.

Rumi discovered poetry and became a Sufi mystic after meeting with a wandering Sufi mystic and dervish, Shams Tabrizi, in 1244. Shams became Rumi's sheik, as he lost interest in the knowledge of the mind and became enchanted by the luminous path of the heart. Rumi expressed his love for Shams through music, dance, and poems, after Shams was killed in Damascus, by the students of Rumi who resented the close relationship they both had. Other accounts dispute this and frame Rumi's jealous son as the murder of Shams. Rumi wrote quatrains (rubayat) and odes (ghazals) with his new illumination of the heart. He named a compilation of ghazals as the Divan-e Shams-e Tabrizi. The Masnavi, his masterpiece, contains 60,000 poems he wrote before his death in Konya, in 1273.

Today ardent admirers of Rumi and heads of state visit his tomb every year on December 17, the anniversary of his death, for a whirling dervish ceremony. This 13th century Sufi poet is one of the most passionate, sensual, and mystic poets in the history of humanity and has been given the honorific name Mevlana. Rumi has been lauded as the "most popular poet" and "best selling poet" in America given how his poems transcend the words they are composed of to irrigate the soul with water droplets of light.

What follows are 277 of some of Rumi's most powerful and illuminating quotes. At their core, Rumi captured the sensuous romance of lover and beloved, the luminous learning passed from sheik to disciple, and the supernatural journey from pain to healing. The quotes transcend the physical words they are written in to become seeds that nourish the heart and soul. Much like each ruby-red seed of a pomegranate bursts with life in the sunlight, so too will these quotes by Rumi burst with Sufi wisdom in the moonlight while reading them with pleasure.

277 Rumi Quotes

1. We carry inside us the wonders we seek outside us.

2. Your heart knows the way. Run in that direction.

3. Stop acting so small. You are the universe in ecstatic motion.

4. Love is the bridge between you and everything.

5. Only from the heart can you touch the sky.

6. Raise your words, not voice. It is rain that grows flowers, not thunder.

7. You are not a drop in the ocean. You are the entire ocean, in a drop.

8. Dancing is not just getting up painlessly, like a leaf blown on the wind; dancing is when you tear your heart out and rise out of your body to hang suspended between the worlds.

9. The minute I heard my first love story, I started looking for you, not knowing how blind that was. Lovers don't finally meet somewhere. They're in each other all along.

10. Be certain that in the religion of Love there are no believers and unbelievers. LOVE embraces all.

11. Set your life on fire. Seek those who fan your flames.

12. In your light I learn how to love. In your beauty, how to make poems. You dance inside my chest where no-one sees you, but sometimes I do, and that sight becomes this art.

13. When you seek love with all your heart you shall find its echo in the universe.

14. Your heart is the size of an ocean. Go find yourself in its hidden depths.

15. The very center of your heart is where life begins – the most beautiful place on earth.

16. The moon stays bright when it doesn't avoid the night.

17. Be a lamp, or a lifeboat, or a ladder. Help someone's soul heal. Walk out of your house like a shepherd.

18. The desire to know your own soul will end all other desires.

19. There is a candle in your heart, ready to be kindled. There is a void in your soul, ready to be filled. You feel it, don't you?

20. I have been a seeker and I still am, but I stopped asking the books and the stars. I started listening to the teaching of my soul.

21. By God, when you see your beauty you will be the idol of yourself.

22. I want to sing like the birds sing, not worrying about who hears or what they think.

23. Close your eyes, fall in love, stay there.

24. There is a voice that doesn't use words, listen.

25. What you seek is seeking you.

26. Let the beauty we love be what we do.

27. The lion is most handsome when looking for food.

28. When you do things from your soul, you feel a river moving in you, a joy.

29. Dance until you shatter yourself.

30. Let yourself become living poetry.

31. Be drunk with love, for love is all that exists.

32. You are searching the world for treasure, but the real treasure is Yourself.

33. When the world pushes you to your knees, you're in the perfect position to pray.

34. Be full of sorrow, that you may become a hill of joy; weep that you may break into laughter.

35. In silence there is eloquence. Stop weaving and see how the pattern improves.

36. Let yourself be silently drawn by the stronger pull of what you really love.

37. Your task is not to seek for love, but merely to seek and find all the barriers within yourself that you have built against it.

38. If light is in your heart, you will find your way home.

39. Sell your cleverness and buy bewilderment. Cleverness is mere opinion. Bewilderment brings intuitive knowledge.

40. What hurts you, blesses you. Darkness is your candle.

41. What is planted in each person's soul will sprout.

42. To praise the sun is to praise your own eyes.

43. Look at the moon in the sky, not the one in the lake.

44. In each moment the fire rages, it will burn away a hundred veils. And carry you a thousand steps toward your goal.

45. With every breath, I plant the seeds of devotion, I am a farmer of the heart.

46. Let us carve gems out of our stony hearts and let them light our path to love.

47. Whoever has heart's doors wide open, could see the sun itself in every atom.

48. Lovers have heartaches that can't be cured by drugs or sleep, or games, but only by seeing their beloved.

49. When someone beats a rug, the blows are not against the rug, but against the dust in it.

50. Beauty surrounds us, but usually we need to be walking in a garden to know it.

51. If you are irritated by every rub, how will your mirror be polished?

52. All that you think is rain is not. Behind the veil angels sometimes weep.

53. My words are like a ship, and the sea is their meaning. Come to me and I will take you to the depths of spirit. I will meet you there.

54. The time has come to turn your heart into a temple of fire.

55. Seek the sound that never ceases. Seek the sun that never sets.

56. The world is a mountain, in which your words are echoed back to you.

57. Be melting snow. Wash yourself of yourself.

58. Laugh as much as your breathe. Love as long as you live.

59. In their seeking, wisdom and madness are one and the same. On the path of love, friend and stranger are one and the same.

60. Two there are who are never satisfied – the lover of the world and the lover of knowledge.

61. Your radiance shines in every atom of creation yet our petty desires keep it hidden.

62. If you want to win hearts, sow the seeds of Love. If you want heaven, stop scattering thorns on the road.

63. Why are you knocking at every door? Go, knock at the door of your own heart.

64. This is what love does and continues to do. It tastes like honey to adults and milk to children.

65. This is love: to fly toward a secret sky, to cause a hundred veils to fall each moment. First to let go of life. Finally, to take a step without feet.

66. Let your teacher be love itself.

67. Whatever happens, just keep smiling and lose yourself in love.

68. On the path of love we are neither masters nor the owners of our lives. We are only a brush in the hand of the master painter.

69. Every moment is made glorious by the light of love.

70. Do not worry if all the candles in the world flicker and die. We have the spark that starts the fire.

71. Tend to your vital heart, and all that you worry about will be solved.

72. Why should I be unhappy? Every parcel of my being is in full bloom.

73. If destiny comes to help you, love will come to meet you. A life without love isn't a life.

74. Oh! Joy for he who has escaped from this world of perfumes and color! For beyond these colors and these perfumes, these are other colors in the heart and the soul.

75. When you feel a peaceful joy, that's when you are near truth.

76. Be grateful for your life, every detail of it, and your face will come to shine like a sun, and everyone who sees it will be made glad and peaceful.

77. Be kind and honest, and harmful poisons will turn sweet inside you.

78. Be a helpful friend, and you will become a green tree with always new fruit, always deeper journeys into love.

79. A warm, rainy day-this is how it feels when friends get together. Friend refreshes friend then, as flowers do each other, in a spring rain.

80. Don't dismiss the heart, even if it's filled with sorrow. God's treasures are buried in broken hearts.

81. Always search for your innermost nature in those you are with, as rose oils imbibes from roses.

82. Join the community of saints and know the delight of your own soul. Enter the ruins for your heart and learn the meaning of humility.

83. If you could get rid of yourself just one, the secret of secrets would open to you. The face of the unknown, hidden beyond the universe would appear on the mirror of your perception.

84. The only lasting beauty is the beauty of the heart.

85. Everything that is made beautiful and fair and lovely is made for the eye of one who sees.

86. The universe and the light of the stars come through me.

87. Whatever happens to you, don't fall in despair. Even if all the doors are closed, a secret path will be there for you that no one knows. You can't see it yet but so many paradises are at the end of this path… Be grateful! It is easy to thank after obtaining what you want, thank before having what you want.

88. Wear gratitude like a cloak and it will feed every corner of your life.

89. The sky will bow down to your beauty, if you do.

90. The beauty you see in me is a reflection of you.

91. What hurts the soul? To live without tasting the water of its own essence.

92. You have no need to travel anywhere – journey within yourself. Enter a mine of rubies and bathe in the splendor of your own light.

93. Who could be so lucky? Who comes to a lake for water and sees the reflection of the moon.

94. Let the waters settle and you will see the moon and the stars mirrored in your own being.

95. Love is the water of life, nurturing heart and soul...

96. Daylight, full of small dancing particles and the one great turning, our souls are dancing with you, without feet, they dance. Can you see them when I whisper in your ear?

97. Truth lifts the heart, like water refreshes thirst.

98. Without love, all worship is a burden, all dancing is a chore, all music is mere noise.

99. Whoever knows the power of dance, knows God.

100. Listen to the sound of waves within you.

101. Dance when you can break yourself up to pieces and totally abandon your worldly passions.

102. Those who don't feel this love pulling them like a river, those who don't drink dawn like a cup of springwater or take in sunset like a supper, those who don't want to change, let them sleep.

103. Sit quietly and listen for a voice that will say, "Be more silent." As that happens, your soul starts to revive.

104. Yesterday I was clever, so I wanted to change the world. Today I am wise, so I am changing myself.

105. Don't be satisfied with stories, how things have gone with others. Unfold your own myth.

106. We came whirling out of nothingness, scattering stars like dust... The stars made a circle, and in the middle, we dance.

107. The wound is the place where the light enters you.

108. You have to keep breaking your heart until it opens.

109. Those pains you feel are messengers. Listen to them.

110. Don't you know yet? It is your light that illuminates the worlds.

111. You've seen my descent. Now watch my rising.

112. Live life as if everything is rigged in your favor.

113. Why are you so enchanted by this world, when a mine of gold lies within you? Open your eyes and come. Return to the root of the root of your own soul.

114. Dance, and make joyous the love around you. Dance, and your veils which hide the Light shall swirl in a heap at your feet.

115. The lamps are different, but the light is the same.

116. Life is a balance between holding on and letting go.

117. Actually, your soul and mine are the same, we appear and disappear in each other.

118. Inside you there's an artist you don't know about.

119. Love is an emerald. Its brilliant light wards off dragons on this treacherous path.

120. You cannot hide love. Love will get on its way to the heart of someone you love. Far or near, it goes home to where it belongs to the heart of lovers.

121. You will learn by reading, but you will understand with LOVE.

122. The garden of the world has no limits, except in your mind.

123. Love is not an emotion, it's your very existence.

124. Love rests on no foundation. It is an endless ocean, with no beginning or end.

125. Everything in the universe is within you. Ask all from yourself.

126. Moonlight floods the whole sky from horizon to horizon; how much it can fill your room depends on its windows.

127. I see my beauty in you.

128. When soul rises into lips you feel the kiss you have wanted.

129. The soul is here for its own joy.

130. Be motivated like the falcon, hunt gloriously. Be magnificent as the leopard, fight to win. Spend less time with nightingales and peacocks. One is all talk, the other only color.

131. Everyone is so afraid of death, but the real Sufis just laugh: nothing tyrannizes their hearts. What strikes the oyster shell does not damage the pearl.

132. Look carefully around you and recognize the luminosity of souls. Sit beside those who draw you to that.

133. This is how I would die into the love I have for you: As pieces of cloud dissolve in sunlight.

134. In the silence of love you will find the spark of life.

135. Come, seek, for search is the foundation of fortune: every success depends upon focusing the heart.

136. Gamble everything for love, if you are a true human being. Half-heartedness does not reach into majesty.

137. You were born with wings, why prefer to crawl through life?

138. Words are a pretext. It is the inner bond that draws one person to another, not words.

139. Let yourself be silently drawn by the stronger pull of what you really love. It will not lead you astray.

140. Don't grieve. Anything you lose comes round in another form.

141. Where there is ruin, there is hope for a treasure.

142. There are a thousand ways to kneel and kiss the earth.

143. It's good to leave each day behind, like flowing water, free of sadness. Yesterday is gone and its tale told. Today new seeds are growing.

144. You dance inside my chest where no one sees you.

145. Being a candle is not easy, in order to give light one must first burn.

146. If you want the moon, do not hide from the night. If you want a rose, do not run from the thorns. If you want love, do not hide from yourself.

147. Half of live is lost in charming others. The other half is lost going through anxieties caused by others. Leave this play, you have played enough.

148. Maybe you are searching among branches for what only appears in the roots.

149. If you only say one prayer in a day, make it "thank you."

150. Soul, if you want to learn secrets, your heart must forget about shame and dignity. You are God's lover, yet you worry what people are saying.

151. Be foolishly in love, because love is all there is.

152. You wander from room to room hunting for the diamond necklace that is already around your neck.

153. I belong to no religion. My religion is love. Every heart is my temple.

154. Not the ones speaking the same language, but the ones sharing the same feeling, understand each other.

155. I closed my mouth and spoke to you in a hundred silent ways.

156. Gratitude is wine for the soul. Go on, get drunk.

157. All your attempts to reach Me, are in reality My attempts to reach you.

158. What hurts you blesses you.

159. Patience is not sitting and waiting, it is foreseeing. It is looking at the thorn and seeing the rose, looking at the night and seeing the day. Lovers are patient and know that the moon needs time to become full.

160. The desire to know your own soul will end all other desires.

161. Listen with ears of tolerance. See through eyes of compassion. Speak with the language of love.

162. With your fragrance in the air, I give my love to the wind.

163. I am another you. You are another me.

164. In this world everything attracts something. Those of the Fire attract those of the Fire; those of the Light attract those of the Light.

165. You are the master alchemist. You light the fire of love in earth and sky, in heart and soul of every human being.

166. Except for love, nothing you see will remain forever.

167. I am a spark form the infinite.

168. Not all storms come to disrupt your life, some come to clear your path.

169. In the house of lovers, the music never stops, the walls are made of songs and the floor dances.

170. Don't wait any longer. Dive in the ocean, leave and let the sea be you.

171. The soul has been given its own ears to hear things the minds doesn't understand.

172. As you live deeper in the heart, the mirror gets cleaner and cleaner.

173. To join the eternal soul, you must become a soul.

174. What you deeply love saves you.

175. Never lose hope my heart. Miracles dwell in the invisible.

176. I learned that every mortal will taste Death. But only some will taste Life.

177. Look at Love with the eyes of your Heart.

178. You say nothing yet I feel the grace of being lost in You.

179. The body is a device for discovering the astronomy of the spirit.

180. Both light and shadow are the dance of love.

181. Be silent, only the hand of God can remove the burdens of your heart.

182. Your spirit is mingled with mine. What touches you, touches me.

183. Giving thanks for abundance is sweeter than the abundance itself.

184. A candle never loses any of its light while lighting another candle.

185. They say there is a doorway from heart to heart, but what is the use of a door when there are no walls?

186. Be a witness not a judge. Focus on yourself, not on others. Listen to your heart, not to the crowd.

187 Love is the flame which, when it blazes consumes everything other than the Beloved.

188. Where the lips are silent, the heart knows a thousand ways to speak.

189. We rarely hear the inward music but we're all dancing to it nevertheless.

190. Tear off the mask. Your face is glorious.

191. I am in love with Love and Love is in love with Me.

192. You are the soul of the soul of the universe, and your name is Love.

193. If you become a helper of hearts, springs of wisdom will flow from your heart.

194. This place is a dream. Only a sleeper considers it real. Then death comes like dawn, and you wake up laughing at what you thought was your grief.

195. Love cannot be described. It must be tasted.

196. Wherever you are, and whatever you do be in love.

197. Your journey is the journey of love. Sense it to its depth and say no more.

198. Deep in our heart, the light of heaven is shining!

199. I am not this hair, I am not this skin, I am the soul that lives within.

200. I looked in temples, churches and mosques. But I found the Divine within my heart.

201. Close your eyes and gaze in the mirror at the flame that lit your senses.

202. Your charm lured me to the edge of madness… I lost my composure!

203. I wrote your name in my Heart and forever it will stay.

204. They will ask you, "what have you produced?" Say to them, "Except for Love, what else can a lover produce?"

205. There is a sacred in tears. They are not the mark of weakness, but of power.

206. With each passing moment a Soul sets off to find itself.

207. You have no need to travel anywhere. Journey within yourself, enter a mine of rubies and bathe in the splendor of your own Light.

208. Silence is the language of God. All else is poor translation.

209. Your soul is so close to mine that what you dream, I know… I know everything you think of: your heart is so close to mine!

210. The heart is cooking a pot of food for you. Be patient until it is cooked.

211. I am a drunkard from another kind of tavern. I dance to a silent tune. I am the symphony of stars.

212. I once had a thousand desires. But in my one desire to know you, all else melted away.

213. I know you're tired but come, this is the way.

214. You are not one you are a Thousand. Just Light your Lantern.

215. To love is human. To feel pain is human. Yet to still love despite the pain is pure angel.

216. Be soulful, be kind, be in love. Love is all there is. Love is the whole thing. We are only pieces.

217. Your heart and my heart are very, very old friends.

218. It is love that holds everything together and it is everything also.

219. God writes spiritual mysteries on our hearts, where they wait silently for discovery.

220. The heart is the secret inside the secret.

221. The heart has its own language. The heart know a hundred thousand ways to speak.

222. I have put the ear of my soul in the window of your heart.

223. Love is like musk. It attracts attention.

224. Love's greatest gift is its ability to make everything it touches sacred.

225. If you have a heart, go, seek a sweetheart.

226. Lovely days don't come to you, you should walk to them.

227. Oh soul, you worry too much. You have seen your own strength. You have seen your own beauty. You have seen your golden wings. Of anything less, why do you worry? You are, in truth, the soul of the soul of the soul.

228. I don't care about marvelous sights! I only want to be in Your presence.

229. I tell you truly, everything you now see will vanish like a dream.

230. There comes a time when nothing is meaningful except surrendering to love.

231. The inspiration you seek is already within you. Be silent and listen.

232. There is a sun within every person.

233. Nothing can nourish the Soul but Light.

234. Only the Soul knows what love is.

235. Close both eyes to see with the other eye.

236. There is a subtle truth: whatever you love, you are.

237. Both light and shadow are the dance of Love.

238. Seek the fountain from within yourself.

239. In the station of Love, you see old men getting younger and younger.

240. Escape the black cloud that surrounds you. Then you will see your own light as radiant as the full moon.

241. When my core is touched by music, Love's wine begins to flow.

242. As you start to walk out of the way, the way appears.

243. Do you run from joy? Perhaps the lion should not flee the fox.

244. You're the road of love and at the end of it is my home.

245. Silence gives Answers.

246. Go find yourself first so you can find me.

247. Shine like the whole universe is yours.

248. When inward tenderness finds the secret hurt, pain itself will crack the rock and ah! Let the soul emerge.

249. It was not into my ear you whispered, but into my heart. It was not my lips you kissed, but my soul.

250. I will be waiting here, for your silence to break, for your soul to shake, for your love to wake.

251. Your body is away from me, but there is a window open from my heart to yours.

252. You and I will be together till the universe dissolves.

253. Play on My Beloved… Let me not miss one note of your melody nor one beat of your heart.

254. When I am silent, I have thunder hidden inside.

255. The lover is ever drunk with love. She is free, he is mad. She sings with delight, as he dances in ecstasy. Caught on our own thoughts we worry about everything but once we get drunk on that love, whatever will be, will be.

256. The quieter you become, the more you are able to hear.

257. Stop the words now, open the window in the center of your chest and let the soul fly in and out.

258. In every religion there is love, yet love has no religion.

259. Keep knocking and the joy inside will eventually open a window and look out to see who's there.

260. Respond to every call that excites your spirit.

261. Let the beauty of what you love be what you do.

262. Goodbyes are only for those who love with their eyes, because for those who love with heart and soul, there is no separation.

263. I am yours. Don't give myself back to me.

264. Listen to silence. It has so much to say.

265. I will soothe you, I will bring you roses. I too have been covered with thorns.

266. Don't sit and wait. Get out there, feel life.

267. I searched for God and found only myself. I searched for myself and found only God.

268. Whenever sorrow comes, be kind to it. For God has placed a pearl in sorrow's hand.

269. Let silence take you to the core of life.

270. With life as short as a half taken breath, don't plant anything but love.

271. Behind every atom of this world hides an infinite universe.

272. There is a fountain inside of you. Don't walk around with an empty bucket.

273. You know how it is. Sometimes we plan a trip to one place, but something takes us to another.

274. The only way to measure a lover is by the grandeur of the beloved.

275. No more holding back. Be reckless. Tell your Love to everybody.

276. The way toward heaven is inward. Lift the wings of love.

277. A heart filled with love is like a phoenix that no cage can imprison.

Pomegranates from Ancient Persia to California

Pomegranates are on of Iran's treasured gifts to the rest of the world. The pomegranate grows wild where it originates in the central Iranian plateau. It is featured as a motif in its arts, dazzling in its famous Persian carpets, ceramics, and poetry. In ancient Persia, it was believed that Eve was tempted with a seductive pomegranate in the Garden of Eden. The ancient Persians revered the pomegranate as a symbol of prosperity, fertility, and rebirth. The followers of Zarathustra included the fruit in religious rites, from marriages to child purification baths to the last rites of a dying Zoroastrian. Luscious red fruits, mainly the pomegranate and the watermelon, are served for the Persian winter solstice, Yalda Night, celebrated by Iranians around the world. In Persian mythology, Esfandiyar the Invincible becomes a hero after he eats a pomegranate, emerging victorious from seven battles: slaying two ravenous wolves, two vicious lions, a formidable dragon, a wicked enchantress, a mythical bird and its chicks, enduring a three-day storm and crossing a desert.

The pomegranate is said to have been grown in the Hanging Gardens of Babylon, one of the Seven Wonders of the Ancient World. In Persian, pomegranates are known as *anar*. In Arabic though, the word for pomegranates is *ruman*, leaving one to wonder whether it derives from

Rumi's name, as both have their roots in Persia and were exported to the rest of the world via the trade caravans. The Koran depicts the pomegranate tree in the Garden of Eden and in the gardens of paradise. Therefore it is regarded as sacred by Muslims. Sheikh Nefzaui of Tunisia, wrote a book on oriental lovemaking in 1500 A.D., in which the pomegranate juice was described as having positive fertility effects. In the *One Thousand and One Nights*, some tales mention "a dish of pomegranate seeds," while in another a once childless sultan fathers fifty children from his fifty concubines after eating fifty seeds from a pomegranate in his garden. Narin Qal'eh in the Iranian city of Meybod is a six story castle that now lies in ruins and used to be called the Castle of Pomegranate (Qal'ehi Anar). Some claim that the Castle of Pomegranate is the castle or white fortress (Dezhe Sefid) depicted in Ferdowsi's Shahnameh.

From its roots in central Iran, the pomegranate

spread to the rest of the Near East and Central Asia. During the Greco-Persian Wars, Persian soldiers, following Xerxes in the campaign to conquer the Greek city states, carried spears adorned with golden and silver pomegranates instead of spikes. The symbolism of the pomegranate spears attested to the Persian Zoroastrian faith. Ultimately though the Persian conquest of Greece failed at the famed battle of Salamis, in 480 B.C. Eastwards, the pomegranate reached India along the Persian Gulf, Arabian Sea, and Indian Ocean maritime trade routes. It reached China through Samarkand via the Silk Road. Westwards, it reached Spain across the Mediterranean Sea from Lebanon and Israel. A region of Spain was called "Grenada" due to the pomegranate gardens that dotted the horizon. The pomegranate reached the New World with Spanish conquistadors and missionaries that landed in Mexico. In California, the pomegranate was introduced by the Spanish settlers in 1769 in the San Joaquin valley. Persians have a love affair with pomegranates using it throughout their flavorful cuisine. The first sherbet, from the Persian *sharbat* was made from snow mixed with pomegranate juice as recorded by Ismail Gorgani in the 12th century Persian book *Zakhireye Khwarazmshahi*. It is said that sherbet was one of Rumi's favorite drinks. The first time I was introduced to the precious luminescent red seeds of the pomegranate was when I was a little boy about 7 years old.

Pomegranates were used more in European cuisine 500 years ago than they are today, according to cookbooks from the period. This culinary reversal in history may be due to the Islamic invasions of Spain and Sicily, when the pomegranate was brought to the conquered kitchens of Southern Europe. The Emir of Granada used the pomegranate as his heraldic emblem, and his emirate is believed to be named after the bright, scarlet fruit. After the fall of the Emirate of Granada and the Emirate of Sicily, the pomegranate fell out of popularity from Europe's epicurean palette. The pomegranate is back in vogue in restaurants in London and Los Angeles (a.k.a. Tehrangeles) as it is incorporated as a bejeweled ingredient of various food items on the menu. Pomegranates are the jewels in the fruit crown due to the widespread use of the ruby red fruit from pomegranate juice, vodka, salad dressing, ice cream, salsa, lollipops, gummy bears, pies, cakes, soups, and rice dishes.

The Pomegranate Garden (Poem by Rumi)

Come to the garden in spring.

There is light and wine,

and sweethearts in the pomegranate blossoms.

If you do not come, these do not matter.

If you do come, these do not matter.

-Rumi

Pomegranate Blossoms (Poem by Rumi)

I said, meet me in the garden.

You know the one-

it is called Smiling Spring.

There are nightingales chirping away,

wine and candle lights,

and companions as soft as

pomegranate blossoms.

You think this all would sound so perfect!

But without you by my side,

what use is the Smiling Spring?

And when you are with me,

what use are

pomegranate blossoms?

-Rumi

Pomegranate Flower Blush (Poem by Rumi)

What was said to the rose that made it open

was said to me here in my heart.

What was told to the cypress

that made it strong and straight,

What was whispered to the jasmine

so that it is what it has become,

Whatever made sugarcane

sweet;

Whatever was said to the dwellers of the town of Chigil

in Turkestan that makes them so beautiful,

Whatever lets the pomegranate

flower blush like a human face,

Those words are being

said to me now. I am blushing.

Whatever put eloquence in language,

that's happening here.

The majestic chamber doors open;

I fill with gratitude,

sucking a piece of sugarcane,

in love with the owner of all these precious things!

-Rumi

The Laughter of Pomegranates (Poem by Rumi)

If you buy a pomegranate,

buy one whose ripeness

has caused it to be cleft open

with a seed-revealing smile.

Its laughter is a blessing,

for through its wide-open mouth

it shows its heart,

like a pearl in the jewel box of spirit.

The red anemone laughs, too,

but through its mouth you glimpse a blackness.

A laughing pomegranate
brings the whole garden to life.
Keeping the company of the holy
makes you one of them
Whether you are stone or marble,
you will become a jewel
when you reach a human being of heart.

Plant the love of the holy ones within your spirit;
don't give your heart to anything
but the love of those whose hearts are glad.
Don't go to the neighborhood of despair:
there is hope.
Don't go in the direction of darkness:
suns exist.

The heart guides you to the neighborhood of the saints;

the body takes you to the prison of water and earth.

Give your heart the food of holy friends;

seek maturity from those who have matured.

-Rumi

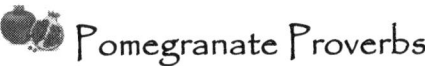 Pomegranate Proverbs

"Eat a pomegranate and visit a bath; your youth will haste back," – Ancient Egyptian Proverb.

"May we be full of merits like the pomegranate (is full of seeds)," Hebrew Proverb.

"A pomegranate never tastes like a fig," – Greek Proverb.

"In every pomegranate a decayed pip is to be found," – Latin Proverb.

"Three pomegranate fell down from heaven: one for the storyteller, one for the listener, and one for the whole world." – Armenian Proverb.

"In every pomegranate, there is one seed that comes from heaven," – Arabic Proverb.

"You can find no pomegranates on a willow tree, nor shame in wicked," –Turkish Proverb.

"A sweet pomegranate will not become bitter, and a bitter pomegranate will not become sweet," Kashmiri Proverb.

"One pomegranate and a hundred sick," Hindi/Urdu Proverb.

"Olive trees don't produce pomegranates," Sicilian Proverb.

"A pomegranate at the side of the road must be sour," Spanish/Valencian Proverb.

"I wish you a long and happy life like Shabe Yalda, sweet as watermelon and fruitful as pomegranates!" – Persian Proverb.

Printed in Great Britain
by Amazon